EPIC BATTLES

ROB COLSON

WAYLAND

CONTENTS

GETTYSBURG

SIEGE OF YORKTOWN

BATTLE OF
BRITAIN

WATERLOO

AGINCOURT

SIEGE OF
STALINGRAD

CANNAE

THE SOMME

TRAFALGAR

LEPANTO

DESERT STORM

THERMOPYLAE
AND SALAMIS

INTRODUCTION

Throughout history, different cultures and civilisations have clashed violently in bloody and brutal battles.

Warriors from opposing forces faced one another on the battlefield in terrifying hand-to-hand fights that were the ultimate test of courage, strength and endurance. The need for better weapons led to new inventions and advances in technology. Today, battles are fought with sophisticated weapons, and soldiers may never actually see their enemies.

The first organised armies appeared in about 2500 BCE in the area known as Mesopotamia, in present-day Iraq. Here, people had settled in large cities for the first time, and these cities came into conflict with one another. Their armies fought battles with spears, axes and daggers. They rode wooden chariots pulled by horses.

SINCE 3600 BCE, THERE HAVE BEEN 14,500 MAJOR WARS, AND NEARLY FOUR BILLION PEOPLE HAVE BEEN KILLED.

By the 20th century, wars were no longer fought between cities but between countries, and even across continents. Advances in technology changed the face of warfare. During World War I, lethal weapons such as rapid-firing machine guns caused large numbers of casualties on the battlefield. The development of aircraft meant that battles were also fought in the air. Modern conflicts have seen a huge rise in the numbers of civilian casualties, in bombing raids and battles fought on the streets of towns and cities.

Many modern armies use expensive weapons technology and much of the fighting is carried out from a distance. In recent years, many armies have used unmanned drones to attack remote targets. The soldiers controlling the drones may be at a base many hundreds of kilometres away.

During World War I, a British soldier had to be over the age of 19. However, more than 250,000 underage soldiers fought for British forces during the war. The youngest soldier was just 12.

SINCE 1945, NEARLY 90 PER CENT OF CASUALTIES IN ARMED CONFLICTS HAVE BEEN CIVILIANS.

THERMOPYLAE AND SALAMIS

Date:	August 480 BCE
Location:	Thessaly, northern Greece, Salamis

THERMOPYLAE:

Forces	Greeks: 7,000; Persians: 130,000
Casualties:	Greeks: 2,500; Persians: 20,000

SALAMIS:

Ships	Greeks: 380; Persians: 1,200
Casualties	Greeks: 40 ships; Persians: 200 ships

Having failed to conquer Greece in 490 BCE, the Persian Empire, under the leadership of Xerxes, invaded Greece again ten years later.

Standing in their way was a small group of Greek city-states, including Athens and Sparta. Vastly outnumbered, the Greeks were beaten in a land battle at Thermopylae in Thessaly, but defeated the much larger Persian fleet at a naval battle at Salamis.

Xerxes led his 130,000-strong army towards Athens through northern Greece, following the coast. On the way, the troops had to march through a narrow pass between the mountains and the sea at Thermopylae. Here, a small group of Greeks, led by the Spartan king Leonidas and 300 of his best men, blocked their path. The Greeks held off the Persian army for three days. Then a Greek traitor told Xerxes of a mountain path around Thermopylae. The Persians took the path and attacked the Greeks from both sides, killing them all.

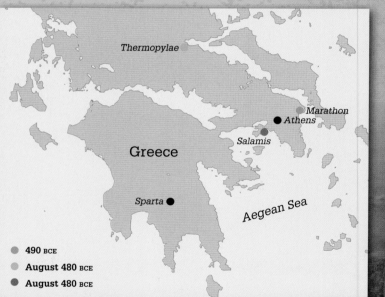

Thermopylae

Marathon
Athens

Salamis

Greece

Sparta

Aegean Sea

- 490 BCE
- August 480 BCE
- August 480 BCE

GREEK SOLDIERS WERE KNOWN AS HOPLITES.

TIMELINE

490 BCE

The first Persian invasion of Greece ends when the Athenians are victorious at the Battle of Marathon.

On hearing of the defeat at Thermopylae, the Greek leader Themistocles set sail with his fleet south to the straits off the island of Salamis. The Greeks tricked the Persians into sailing after them, and trapped the Persian ships in the narrow straits. After seven hours of battle, the Persians were defeated. With winter approaching, the Persians had no choice but to leave Greece, whose independence was now safe.

This statue of Leonidas, who died at Thermopylae, shows the Spartan king wearing a helmet with a horsehair crest and carrying a shield decorated with the head of a monster called a gorgon.

WEAPONS OF WAR

Greek warships were called triremes. They had sails, but were also powered by three lines of oars on either side. Up to 170 men rowed the oars. Lacking guns or cannons, the triremes defeated enemy ships by ramming into them. Soldiers would then jump onto the enemy ships and fight at close quarters using spears and axes.

All male citizens of the city of Sparta trained to be soldiers from the age of seven. The training involved great physical hardship, and the boys were encouraged to fight one another. The Spartan hoplites were feared across Greece for their discipline and fighting skills.

481 BCE

The Persian emperor Xerxes orders the Greeks to surrender, but the Greeks decide to fight the Persian invaders.

AUG 480 BCE

The Persians defeat the Greeks at the Battle of Thermopylae.

AUG 480 BCE

The Persian fleet is defeated at Salamis by the Greeks, and the Persians retreat.

CANNAE

A CRUSHING DEFEAT FOR ROME

Date:	2 August 216 BCE
Location:	Cannae, southern Italy
Forces:	Romans: 80,000; Carthaginians: 50,000
Casualties:	Romans: 50,000 killed, 15,000 taken prisoner; Carthaginians: 6,000 killed

During the 200s BCE, two great powers, Rome and Carthage, fought for control of the Mediterranean Sea in a series of conflicts called the Punic Wars.

In 216 BCE, at Cannae in southern Italy, the Carthaginians inflicted a huge defeat on the Romans on one of the deadliest days in the history of warfare.

Two years before the battle, the Carthaginian leader, Hannibal, led his forces on a long journey through Spain and France and over the Alps into Italy. His army had 100,000 men, and even included elephants.

Gaul · Alps · Alps · Alps · Spain · Lake Trasimene · Rome · Cannae · Mediterranean Sea · AFRICA · Carthage · Zama

- 220 BCE
- 218 BCE
- 217 BCE
- 216 BCE
- 202 BCE

The son of a Carthaginian general, Hannibal spent a great deal of his life fighting or plotting against Rome. After his defeat at Zama, he went on to help Syrian forces in their conflict against Rome, but he was unsuccessful again. Pursued by the Romans, he eventually committed suicide around 183 BCE.

FEWER THAN 15,000 ROMAN SOLDIERS MANAGED TO ESCAPE FROM THE BATTLE.

TIMELINE

218 BCE

The Second Punic War between Rome and Carthage begins as Hannibal marches his army across the Alps into Northern Italy.

Just 20,000 men survived the journey, but they were joined along the way by Gauls from France. As his army marched south, Hannibal inflicted many defeats on the Romans, such as at Lake Trasimene. When he captured a major supply route at Cannae in southern Italy, the Romans sent a huge army to destroy him.

WEAPONS OF WAR

Elephants could be devastating weapons, crushing any opposition with powerful charges. However, they could not turn very well. At the Battle of Zama, the Roman forces simply moved out of their way, letting them charge through harmlessly.

Both sides faced each other close to the River Aufidus. The Romans advanced and pushed back the centre of the Carthaginian army. However, the flanks, or sides, of Hannibal's army swept around to encircle the Romans. Completely surrounded and unable to escape, the Romans were massacred.

Despite his victory, Hannibal did not march on Rome. Fourteen years after Cannae, the Romans, led by the Roman general Scipio, landed in North Africa. **This forced Hannibal to return and he was defeated at the Battle of Zama.**

217 BCE
Hannibal defeats the Roman army at Lake Trasimene.

2 AUGUST 216 BCE
The Carthaginians inflict a massive defeat on the Romans at Cannae.

202 BCE
The Second Punic War ends as Hannibal is defeated by Scipio at Zama in North Africa.

AGINCOURT

VICTORY AGAINST THE ODDS

Date:	25 October 1415
Location:	Agincourt, France
Forces:	English: 6,000; French: 60,000
Casualties:	French: 7,000 dead; English: 500 dead or wounded

In northern France in 1415, the English king Henry V pulled off a stunning victory against a huge French army.

Henry had invaded France in what looked to be a hopeless cause, and his tired and hungry troops were outnumbered ten to one. However, a combination of tactical genius and luck won the day. In heavy rain, the narrow battlefield quickly turned into a mud bath. This slowed the advance of the French, who moved forwards under a barrage of arrows. The English had driven a line of wooden stakes into the ground. French horsemen at the front were impaled on them.

England

English Channel

Agincourt

Harfleur

Normandy

France

1413

22 Sept 1415

25 Oct 1415

TIMELINE

1413

Henry V becomes king of England. He maintains a claim to the French throne.

AUG 1415

Henry lands in Normandy to claim the French throne.

English king Henry V was closely related to the French royal family, and invaded France in an attempt to unite the English and French crowns. The Battle of Agincourt formed part of the Hundred Years' War, in which a series of English and French kings fought for control of each other's kingdoms.

From behind the stakes, English archers rained down a shower of arrows. The second line of French soldiers had to climb over their dead comrades and soon became stuck in the mud, where the English could easily kill them. Seeing the disaster ahead of them, the third line of French soldiers decided not to attack, and Henry won the battle.

WEAPONS OF WAR

The longbow was first used by the Welsh in battles with the English. The English army adopted it after seeing how deadly it could be. The longbow played a crucial role in Henry's victory at Agincourt. The bow was as tall as a man and very powerful. It could hit a target up to 300 m (1,000 ft) away. Archers spent many years training to build up the strength and skills needed and a good archer could shoot up to ten arrows in a minute.

THE FRENCH WERE FINISHED OFF BY ENGLISH SOLDIERS USING AXES AND SWORDS.

With such a small army, Henry decided that he could not guard any prisoners, and captured French soldiers were killed. By the end of the battle, more than 90 French noblemen, including their commander Charles d'Albret, lay dead.

22 SEPT 1415
Henry takes the city of Harfleur after a long siege. His men are now hungry and tired.

25 OCT 1415
The English defeat the French at the Battle of Agincourt.

1420
Henry is recognised as the heir to the French throne. Henry is never made king of France, but later English kings continue to claim France as theirs.

LEPANTO
STOPPING THE OTTOMAN EMPIRE

Date:	**7 October 1571**
Location:	**Gulf of Patras, Greece**
Forces:	**Ottomans: 50,000; Holy League: 80,000**
Casualties:	**Ottomans: 15,000–20,000 dead; Holy League: 7,566 dead**

In 1571, two huge fleets of ships clashed in the narrow straits of the Gulf of Patras in Western Greece, in a decisive battle between Christian and Muslim forces.

The Muslim Ottomans, under Emperor Selim II, had been pushing west in a series of bloody conquests, including Cyprus in 1570. A 'Holy League' of Christian forces, made up of several different nations, was assembled by Pope Pius V to stop the invaders from conquering the whole of Europe.

The two fleets faced each other, spread out across 8 km (5 miles) of sea. The Holy League fleet was led by six galleasses, a new kind of galley twice the size of other ships in the fleet. They each carried 40 large cannons.

Venice · Rome · Messina · *Ottoman Empire* · Lepanto · Gulf of Patras · Cyprus

● 1570
● 7 October 1571

Don John of Austria succeeded in bringing together the fleets of Spain, Venice and the papal navy into one effective fighting force so that they could defeat the Ottoman fleet.

TIMELINE

1570
The Ottomans capture the island of Cyprus. Pope Pius gathers together a 'Holy League' to fight the Ottomans.

7 OCTOBER 1571
The Holy League defeats the Ottomans at the Battle of Lepanto. The Ottoman fleet is destroyed.

1572
The Ottomans rebuild their fleet, but do not try to invade Europe again for many years.

12

The galleasses broke through the Ottoman lines, with the rest of the Christian fleet following behind. The Ottomans, armed largely with bows and arrows, were no match for the Christians, who had firearms.

The Holy League cannons sunk ship after ship. The Holy League flagship *Real*, under the command of Don John of Austria, rammed the Ottoman flagship and killed the Ottoman commander, Ali Mouezinzade.

WEAPONS OF WAR

Rowing the galleys was hard work in harsh conditions. Many of the Holy League galleys were rowed by convicts. The Ottoman galleys were rowed by slaves, often Christians who had been taken prisoner in earlier battles. Their 251 ships were rowed by a total of 37,000 slaves. As the Ottomans began to lose the battle, the slaves turned on their masters and helped the Holy League soldiers to butcher them. At the end of the battle, 15,000 Christian slaves had been freed.

The Ottomans returned home to Constantinople to inform Selim of their defeat. The Holy League celebrated a famous victory that destroyed the Ottoman fleet. **The battle was widely seen as having saved Christian Europe, and the Ottomans would not attempt to invade again for 70 years.**

ONLY 50 OTTOMAN SHIPS ESCAPED THE BATTLE.

SIEGE OF YORKTOWN

VICTORY FOR THE AMERICANS

Date:	29 September–19 October 1781
Location:	Yorktown, Virginia, America
Forces:	American: 8,845; French: 7,800; British: 7,500
Casualties:	American: 108; French: 186; British: 482 (and 7,018 taken prisoner)

In 1776, 13 American colonies declared themselves independent and broke free from British rule. The resulting war was decided by a victory to American and French forces over the British in a siege of the port of Yorktown.

In 1781, the American commander, George Washington, appeared to be preparing to attack New York to the north of Yorktown, with the help of his French allies. In secret, he sent a message to the French Admiral François de Grasse to sail south instead. Meanwhile, Washington set up dummy camps near New York to fool the British into thinking that he was about to attack. In reality, he was moving his troops south towards Yorktown. The British realised the deception too late to send reinforcements. The British commander at Yorktown, the Earl Cornwallis, had assembled a large force

The American commander-in-chief George Washington, who led the siege of Yorktown, went on to become the first president of the United States.

24 FRENCH SHIPS STOPPED BRITISH HELP ARRIVING BY SEA.

TIMELINE

1776
Thirteen American colonies sign a Declaration of Independence from the British and create the USA.

6 OCTOBER 1781
American and French troops and ships start to lay siege to Yorktown.

at the port to await supplies from the British Royal Navy. But the supplies never came, and he found himself surrounded by the Americans and French. The French blockaded Yorktown from the sea, while a combined force of American and French troops attacked from the land. However, Cornwallis had fortified the port with cannons, making it hard to defeat, and a siege began on 6 October.

The British held out for almost two weeks before their defences started to crumble, and Cornwallis surrendered on 19 October.

WEAPONS OF WAR

Both sides used long flintlock rifles. Although they were not very accurate, they could be used very effectively when fired in a tight mass and they were more reliable than their matchlock predecessors. Long bayonets were also fitted to create a fearsome defensive wall.

Losses on both sides were relatively low. However, the loss of such an important fort led the British to begin peace negotiations. **Two years later, a peace treaty was signed and the war came to an end.**

andée par Mylord Comte de Cornwallis aux Armées Combinées des Etats unis de L'Amérique et de France aux ordres des Generaux Washington et de Rochambeau à Yorck toumn 1781 Il s'est trouvés dans ces deux postes 6000 hommes de troupes reglées Angloises ou Hessoises et 22 Drapeaux 1500 Matelots 160 Canons de tout Calibre dont 75 de Fonte & Mortiers ns qui a été Brulé 20 Coules Bas : Ce jour a jamais memorables pour les Etats unis en ce quil afsura definitivement leurs independances

Yorck Toum | C · Armée Angloise sortant de la place | E Armée Francoise | G Armée naval de France aux Ordres du Comte de Grace | I Riviere d'Yorck
Glocester | D · Les Armes des ennems posée en Faisceaux | F Armée Americaune | H Baye de Chesapeack | A Paris chez Montluc rue S. Jean de Beauvais prés des Jacops

19 OCTOBER 1781

The British are forced to surrender at Yorktown.

1783

A peace treaty is signed to end the American Revolution as Britain gives up its claim to the USA.

TRAFALGAR

NELSON'S HEROIC VICTORY

Date:	21 October 1805
Location:	Near Cape Trafalgar, southern Spain
Forces:	British: 27 ships of the line (see Weapons of War); French/Spanish: 33 ships of the line
Casualties:	British: 449 killed; French/Spanish: 4,408 killed

In six years since coming to power in France, Napoleon Bonaparte had achieved a series of victories across Europe and looked set to dominate the continent.

In 1805, however, Napoleon was forced to abandon plans to invade Britain following a naval battle at Trafalgar, where the British admiral Horatio Nelson inflicted a heavy defeat on a combined French and Spanish fleet.

The French commander, Admiral Pierre Villeneuve, was ordered to gather a fleet to help Napoleon with his planned invasion of Britain. Villeneuve gathered his ships near Cádiz in southern Spain, only to find Nelson waiting for him outside the port. Villeneuve did not want to fight, but Nelson attacked before he had the chance to retreat, and a bloody, day-long battle began.

Nelson himself led the attack in his flagship *Victory*. He had a reputation for bravery, and had lost an eye and an arm in previous battles. In the early afternoon, *Victory* sailed through enemy lines and was attacked by the French ship *Redoutable*.

THE BRITISH CAPTURED 20,000 PRISONERS.

Men clinging to the masts of the French ships rained down gunfire onto the deck of *Victory*, killing many on board, including Nelson himself.

Not knowing that their commander was dead, the British fleet fought on and the battle developed into a brutal hand-to-hand combat. The French suffered terrible losses and many ships were badly damaged. The battle finally ended when the French ship *Achille* caught fire and exploded, causing a huge loss of life. This prompted Villeneuve to surrender.

By the Battle of Trafalgar, Horatio Nelson was already a respected naval commander. He had recorded important victories against the French at the Battle of Cape St Vincent in 1797 and the Battle of the Nile in 1798.

WEAPONS OF WAR

Nelson's ship, HMS *Victory*, was a kind of warship known as a 'ship of the line', the most powerful ship of the time. It had three decks, was fitted with around 50 large cannons, and needed a crew of 850 men. In total, more than 6,000 trees were felled to build the *Victory*.

On hearing of the defeat, Napoleon was furious that he had to abandon his planned invasion. He quickly rebuilt his navy, but power at sea now lay with the British.

TIMELINE

1799
Napoleon Bonaparte comes to power in France.

1805
Napoleon plans an invasion of Britain, and sends Admiral Villeneuve to gather a fleet.

21 OCTOBER 1805
Defeat of Villeneuve by Nelson at Trafalgar puts an end to Napoleon's plan.

WATERLOO

THE END FOR NAPOLEON

Date:	18 June 1815
Location:	Waterloo, south of Brussels
Forces:	British: 67,000; Prussians: 53,000; French: 74,000
Casualties:	British: 15,000; Prussians: 7,000; French: 25,000

Ten years after the naval defeat at Trafalgar, Napoleon suffered a final, decisive defeat at Waterloo. The French faced a force of British and Prussian armies.

Napoleon decided to fight the British and Prussians before their allies, the Austrians and Russians, could join them.

Waterloo was the third battle in as many days, all of which took place in Belgium. The first battle occurred at Ligny, where Napoleon defeated the Prussians, but they managed to escape, which was to prove crucial. The next day, the French confronted the British at Quatre-Bras, where the British held out before withdrawing. Napoleon followed the British, determined to push them north and back to the sea.

Great Britain

Belgium · Waterloo

Paris ●

France

● 16–18 June 1815

Napoleon waited until about midday to start his attack. This was to allow the ground to dry after a heavy rainstorm the night before. **The delay gave the Prussian forces enough time to reach the battlefield later that day.**

8,000 FRENCH SOLDIERS WERE TAKEN PRISONER.

TIMELINE

16 JUNE 1815

French and Prussian forces clash at Ligny, Belgium. The French army wins, but the Prussian force is able to escape.

17 JUNE 1815

The French army fights British soldiers at Quatre-Bras.

The British commander, the Duke of Wellington, decided to confront Napoleon just south of the village of Waterloo. The French attacked the British in a series of exhausting charges, each of which killed many men on both sides. The British held firm until, at 8 o'clock in the evening, their Prussian allies arrived. By then, nearly a third of Napoleon's soldiers had been killed or wounded, and the sight of another army gathering to attack them proved too much. The French army fled, and Napoleon escaped back to Paris.

Napoleon Bonaparte seized power in France in 1799. Over the next 16 years, he fought many military campaigns across Europe in what became known as the Napoleonic Wars. Defeat at Waterloo brought an end to Napoleon's power. He was sent into exile on the island of St Helena in the Atlantic Ocean.

WEAPONS OF WAR

Soldiers mounted on horseback, or cavalry, had been used for thousands of years before the Battle of Waterloo. But their effectiveness was declining due to improvements in firearms. Even so, horse-mounted units remained in use until World War II. Today, horses have been replaced with armoured vehicles and helicopters.

NAPOLEON DIED IN 1821, AFTER SIX YEARS IN EXILE.

18 JUNE 1815

French forces face their third battle in as many days, this time at Waterloo. Napoleon loses and goes into exile.

1821

Napoleon dies in exile on the island of St Helena.

GETTYSBURG

AMERICA'S BLOODIEST BATTLE

Date:	1–3 July 1863
Location:	Gettysburg, Pennsylvania
Forces:	Union: 85,000; Confederate: 75,000
Casualties:	Union: 23,000; Confederate: 28,000

In 1861, a civil war broke out in the USA. Eleven slave-owning states in the south attempted to break away from the rest of the country.

War broke out between the Confederacy in the south and the Union in the north. The war was won by the Union in 1865, and slavery in the USA was abolished. The bloodiest battle of the war took place in 1863 near the town of Gettysburg in Pennsylvania, one of the states on the Union side.

Confederate general Robert E. Lee invaded Pennsylvania in May 1863 in an attempt to force the Union to end the war. He was pursued by a Union army led by Major General George Meade. The two sides first clashed at Gettysburg on 1 July. The Confederates pushed the Union soldiers back, but the Union infantry held onto a strong position on high ground to the south of the town, where they were reinforced. The next day, Lee ordered an attack, but after desperate fighting, he failed to push the Union troops back.

New York

Gettysburg

United States of America

July 1863

Gettysburg was not the largest battle of the civil war. The Battle of Fredericksburg in December 1862 featured nearly 200,000 soldiers from both sides. **The battle ended with a crushing defeat for the Union forces.**

120 GENERALS WERE AT THE BATTLE.

1861	**JULY 1863**	**APRIL 1865**
Eleven southern slave-owning states leave the Union, starting a Civil War.	The Union defeats the Confederates at Gettysburg, sending General Lee's army back to Virginia.	General Lee surrenders and other Confederate forces soon follow his example.

TIMELINE

On 3 July, Lee ordered another attack, and at 3 pm a force of 14,000 Confederate infantry advanced across open fields, where they made easy targets for Union guns. Only a few hundred Confederate soldiers reached the Union line. The battle was over after just half an hour, with thousands of men from both sides lying dead or dying on the ground.

General Lee was forced to take his remaining troops back to Confederate territory. His invasion had failed and within two years the Confederate forces had surrendered and the war was over.

On 19 November 1863, a few months after the battle, United States president Abraham Lincoln gave a speech at Gettysburg. In the speech, which came to be known as the Gettysburg Address, Lincoln committed himself to winning the war in order to bring equality to all citizens. The speech was the first clear signal that Lincoln planned to end slavery across the USA.

WEAPONS OF WAR

Cannons used during the US civil war were pulled around the battlefield by horses. This allowed them to set up at key locations decided by the generals, fire their shots and then move rapidly to the next location.

26 APRIL 1865

The war ends with victory to the Union.

ONE BOMBARDMENT INVOLVED 400 CANNONS.

THE SOMME

SLAUGHTER IN THE MUD

Date:	1 July–18 November 1916
Location:	Northeastern France
Forces:	99 Allied divisions; 50 German divisions
Casualties:	British and Commonwealth: 420,000; French: 200,000; Germans: 500,000

World War I broke out in Europe in 1914 and quickly developed into a bloody stalemate. Casualties were very high on both sides and neither seemed able to gain an advantage.

In 1916, the British and French planned a major offensive against the Germans in northern France. The Battle of the Somme was one of the costliest battles of the war, but came no closer to breaking the deadlock.

The British commanding officer, General Douglas Haig, planned to destroy German defences with artillery, then send in the infantry to take the German lines. On 1 July, British soldiers were ordered 'over the top' of their trenches. However, the bombardment failed, German lines were protected by barbed wire, and the advancing British troops were mown down by fire from machine guns.

Map labels: Great Britain; English Channel; Belgium; Germany; The Somme; Paris; France; Switzerland; July–Nov 1916; Italy

MORE THAN 20,000 BRITISH SOLDERS WERE KILLED ON THE FIRST DAY.

TIMELINE

1914

World War I breaks out in Europe with Germany and Austria-Hungary on one side and Russia, France and Britain on the other.

1916

By 1916, lines of defensive trenches had been dug from the English Channel to the Swiss border in the south. Each side was struggling to advance.

Over the following months, each side launched failed attacks on the other. The last action of the battle, which started on 13 November, saw the British capture the German lines at Beaumont Hamel, which had been one of Haig's objectives on the very first day.

The Battle of the Somme ended in stalemate. Modern technology meant that old battlefield tactics were no longer effective. Advancing lines of infantry were no match for the machine guns and artillery of the enemy. The war ended in 1918, by which time millions of men had been killed.

The Thiepval Memorial in the Somme region was built to remember more than 72,000 British and Commonwealth missing troops who died at the Battle of the Somme. Their bodies were never recovered.

The Battle of the Somme saw the first use of tanks in action. In September 1916, British tanks were used against German positions at Flers-Courcelette. Britain went on to build more than 2,500 tanks during World War I.

WEAPONS OF WAR

On the Western Front, each side dug trenches in which the soldiers remained out of the way of enemy fire. The trenches formed defensive lines, separated by an area known as 'no man's land'. They were protected by barbed wire and machine guns, making them hard to attack, and each major offensive resulted in massive casualties. Soldiers advancing from the trenches were killed in their hundreds of thousands by machine guns, shells, mines and poisonous gas.

JULY–NOVEMBER 1916

At the Somme, more than 1 million men die as the British and French attack but fail to advance.

11 NOVEMBER 1918

An armistice is signed to end World War I. About 16 million men lie dead as a result of the war.

BATTLE OF BRITAIN

VICTORY IN THE SKIES

Date:	July–October 1940
Location:	The skies above Southern England
Forces:	British: 900 fighter planes at the start; Germans: 1,464 fighter planes, 1,380 bombers at the start
Casualties:	British: 1,023 aircraft; Germans: 1,887 aircraft

Less than a year after the start of World War II, German forces had conquered a huge part of Europe. Only Britain stood in the way of a complete victory in western Europe.

German forces massed in northern France to prepare for an invasion of Britain. However, before crossing the English Channel, Hitler needed to destroy Britain's Royal Air Force (RAF). The ensuing air battle became known as the Battle of Britain.

The battle took place through the summer and autumn months of 1940. The German air force, the Luftwaffe, aimed to destroy British fighters before bombing military targets in southern England. This would weaken British defences and prepare the way for invasion.

England
London
English Channel
France
Paris

TIMELINE

1 SEPTEMBER 1939

Adolf Hitler's Germany invades Poland, and World War II starts as Britain and France declare war.

MAY–JUNE 1940

Germany occupies France after winning the Battle of France.

JULY–OCTOBER 1940

The British RAF and the German Luftwaffe fight for control of the skies in the Battle of Britain.

WEAPONS OF WAR

The Spitfire was the RAF's most successful fighter plane during World War II. It was a single-seater, so the pilot had to both fly the plane and operate its guns. The most successful Spitfire pilot of all, Johnnie Johnson, shot down 34 German planes. Johnson made a total of 700 flights during the war.

If Germany could win the fight to control the skies, they looked set to win the war. The British used radar to detect formations of German planes in the skies. This allowed them to concentrate their forces in the correct places.

Every day, British Spitfire and Hurricane fighters appeared to stop the German attacks. By September, the Luftwaffe had switched their attacks from air bases to London, but the Germans continued to lose aircraft. On 15 September, one-quarter of the attacking German planes were shot down or damaged. Two days later, Hitler abandoned his planned invasion. The battle had been won by the British, and Hitler had suffered his first defeat of the war.

DURING THE BLITZ, GERMAN AIRCRAFT DROPPED NEARLY 14,000 TONNES OF BOMBS ON LONDON ALONE.

Having failed to invade and defeat Britain, Hitler turned his attention to the Soviet Union. He committed huge numbers of troops and resources to this invasion. This proved costly as his forces now became stretched.

Large parts of London and many other British cities were destroyed during the German bombing raids.

SEPTEMBER 1940–MAY 1941

On losing the battle, Hitler calls off his planned invasion.

German aircraft bomb British cities, killing 43,000 people. This period is known as the Blitz, after the German word for lightning.

SIEGE OF STALINGRAD

BATTLE IN THE RUINS

Date:	September 1942–2 February 1943
Location:	Stalingrad, Soviet Union
Forces:	Germans: 500,000; Soviets: more than 1 million
Casualties:	Germans: 500,000; Soviets: 750,000

In 1941, two years after the outbreak of World War II, Adolf Hitler's Germany invaded the Soviet Union.

By June 1942, German troops had reached Stalingrad, a major industrial city on the River Volga, now known as Volgograd. A ferocious battle to control the city raged for five months.

June 1941
January 1942
September 1942–
February 1943

Moscow

Soviet Union

Stalingrad

Black Sea

The Germans attacked Stalingrad from the ground and the air, reducing many buildings to rubble. They drove the Soviet defenders back to a narrow strip of land next to the river. With the city in ruins, fighting became a desperate, face-to-face struggle from one building to the next and even from room to room. Led by a young general called Vasili Chuikov, the Soviet forces held out.

As the fight inside Stalingrad continued, Soviet troops surrounded the city, trapping the Germans. With supplies cut off and winter setting in, they were in a desperate situation. Frostbitten, starving and running short of ammunition, the Germans finally surrendered on 30 January.

WEAPONS OF WAR

Both sides used snipers, who hid in the ruined buildings and picked off their enemies one by one. Anyone who had to cross the street was a target. The top Soviet sniper, Vasili Zaitsev, killed more than 200 Germans during the battle.

TIMELINE

JUNE 1941
Adolf Hitler's Germany invades the Soviet Union in Operation Barbarossa.

JANUARY 1942
Soviet troops manage to defend Moscow from German invaders.

FEBRUARY 1943
German troops are surrounded and captured at Stalingrad.

All fighting stopped three days later. More than 1 million people had been killed in the battle, and the city lay in ruins. The defence of Stalingrad marked a major turning point in the war, as the Germans suffered a defeat from which they would never recover.

SOLDIERS FACED TEMPERATURES AS LOW AS -30°C (-20°F).

In honour of the people who fought and died during the Battle of Stalingrad, a huge statue called 'The Motherland Calls' was built on a hill overlooking the city. When it was dedicated in 1967, the 87-m (279-feet) high statue was the tallest in the world.

91,000 GERMAN PRISONERS WERE CAPTURED ALIVE AT THE END OF THE BATTLE.

MAY 1945

World War II ends in Europe as Soviet troops enter the German capital Berlin. Hitler kills himself before he can be captured.

The population of Stalingrad fell from 850,000 before the war, to just 1,500 at the end of the conflict. The last surviving German prisoner of war in the Soviet Union was not returned to his home country until 1956.

DESERT STORM

Date:	January–February 1991
Location:	Kuwait
Forces:	International coalition: 680,000 Iraqis: unknown
Casualties:	International coalition: 1,378 Iraqis: 22,000; Civilians: 2,300

In August 1990, Iraq invaded the small neighbouring country of Kuwait.

In the months that followed, the United Nations tried to persuade Iraq to withdraw. The Iraqi leader, Saddam Hussein, refused to do so, and in January 1991, an international coalition force led by the USA gathered to force Iraq out of Kuwait. The operation was called 'Desert Storm'.

The battle started with a sustained bombardment from the air, codenamed 'Instant Thunder'. In all, the coalition made 110,000 flights over Kuwait, knocking out key targets, such as military headquarters and radar facilities, in order to weaken the Iraqi defences. The US forces used state-of-the-art technology, such as thermal imaging and weapon-locator systems, which allowed them to hit their targets.

TIMELINE

AUG 1990
Iraq invades its neighbour Kuwait and claims it as the 19th province of Iraq.

24 FEB 1991
After a six-week bombing campaign, a coalition force attacks the Iraqis in Kuwait.

3 MARCH 1991
The war officially ends, with the Iraqis forced out of Kuwait.

NOV 1991
The final fires in Kuwait's oil wells are put out.

After four weeks of bombing, the ground attack began on 24 February. A total of 575,000 troops advanced on the weakened Iraqi forces. With superior numbers and technology, the coalition was able to clear the whole of Kuwait of Iraqi forces in just four days.

About 22,000 Iraqi soldiers were killed during the war, while the coalition lost just 1,378. Operation Desert Storm had clearly shown how superior technology could win a battle.

WEAPONS OF WAR

The US used F-117 'Stealth' fighters to hit key targets. These aircraft are specially shaped to make them hard to detect by radar. They are also able to hide the heat coming from their jets, making them hard to spot with heat detectors.

The Iraqis set fire to 700 oil wells as they withdrew from Kuwait. It took nearly a year to put out all the fires. The months of burning caused widespread pollution, and the smoke caused breathing problems for people living in the region.

SOLDIERS IN THE COALITION CAME FROM 39 COUNTRIES.

Twelve years after the Gulf War, Iraq was involved in another conflict in 2003. Forces from the USA, the UK, Australia and Poland invaded the country to depose Saddam Hussein. The Iraqi government was toppled in just 21 days.

THE COST OF THE WAR HAS BEEN PUT AT US$61 BILLION.

HALL oF FAME

BATTLE OF GAUGAMELA

This battle, in 331 BCE, proved a decisive victory for Alexander the Great over the much larger Persian army under the command of Darius III, and led to the fall of the Persian Empire.

SIEGE OF CONSTANTINOPLE

After a siege lasting for seven weeks in 1453, Ottoman forces captured the city of Constantinople, marking the fall of the Byzantine Empire.

BATTLE OF HASTINGS

With a claim to the English throne, William of Normandy invaded in 1066 and defeated Saxon forces led by King Harold II. His victory marked the start of Norman rule in England.

BATTLE OF NASEBY

Fought in 1645, this proved to be the decisive battle of the English Civil War with victory for Parliamentarian forces led by Oliver Cromwell and Sir Thomas Fairfax over the Royalist army commanded by King Charles I.

BATTLE OF SEKIGAHARA

Fought in 1600, victory led to the establishment of the Tokugawa Shogunate (dynasty), which controlled Japan for nearly 300 years.

BATTLE OF AUSTERLITZ

This battle took place in 1805 and is thought to be Napoleon Bonaparte's greatest victory. After nine hours of fighting, French forces defeated a combined army made up of Russian and Austrian soldiers.

BATTLE OF MANASSAS

Also called the First Battle of Bull Run, this was the first major battle of the American Civil War. Fought in 1861, Confederate forces managed to defeat a Union army.

BATTLE OF VERDUN

Fought between February and December 1916, this was the longest battle of World War I and saw the German army attack the French in huge numbers. However, the German forces failed in their objectives.

BATTLE OF MIDWAY

This was one of the most important naval battles in world history and saw the US navy inflict a decisive defeat on the Japanese. Fought in June 1942, American forces stopped the Japanese from capturing the island of Midway in the middle of the Pacific Ocean. The Japanese lost four aircraft carriers and a heavy cruiser, while the Americans lost a single carrier and a destroyer.

BATTLE OF BAGRATION

This offensive saw Soviet forces drive the German army out of most of the Soviet Union between June and August 1944. German casualties numbered more than 500,000 and it was one of the most disastrous defeats for Nazi forces during World War II.

TET OFFENSIVE

Launched in January 1968, this was a surprise attack on a number of military bases, towns and cities by Communist forces against South Vietnamese and US forces during the Vietnam War. After initial victories, the Communists were driven back.

GLOSSARY

ARMISTICE
This is an agreement between two fighting forces to stop hostilities. It might not be the end of a conflict, but it does give both sides a chance to negotiate a formal peace agreement.

BLITZ
A shortening of the German word 'blitzkrieg', meaning 'lightning war', this was a period during the Battle of Britain when the German air force bombed British cities.

BOMBARDMENT
This is a sustained attack by artillery or bomber aircraft on a target.

BAYONET
A long blade that is attached to the muzzle of a rifle to create a spear.

CAVALRY
Units of an army that used to be mounted on horses. Today, cavalry units use armoured vehicles or helicopters.

CHARIOTS
Wheeled vehicles that were pulled into battle by horses or cattle. Soldiers standing on the chariot could attack opponents using bows and arrows or spears.

COALITION
A group made up of different parties who have joined together to complete an objective.

DRONE
An unmanned robot aircraft, which either controls itself or is guided by a pilot situated at a distant location.

EXILE
To be sent out of your own country.

FLANKS
The sides of a formation.

FLEET
A group of planes or ships.

GALLEASSES
These were large merchant ships that were converted into warships. They were powered by oars and sails and armed with cannons.

GALLEYS
Long thin ships that were powered mainly using oars and did not need the wind to move and change direction.

HOPLITES
Ancient Greek soldiers who were usually armed with long spears and shields. They formed tight units called phalanxes.

MACHINE GUN
A type of weapon that is designed to fire a continuous burst of bullets with a single squeeze of the trigger.

RIFLE
The inside of the barrel on this long firearm has spiral grooves, called rifling. These cause a bullet to spin, making it fly more accurately.

SHIP OF THE LINE
A type of warship that was designed to sail in a line formation so that they could deliver a powerful bombardment called a broadside.

SIEGE
When an armed force blocks access to a town, city, area or fortress.

TREATY
A formal agreement between several groups. A peace treaty marks the end of a violent conflict.

TRENCH
A slim ditch that is used as a defensive position. During World War I, enormous trench networks were used by both sides to create a period of stalemate.

TRIREME
An ancient Greek ship that was powered by more than 150 oars arranged in three rows.

INDEX

First published in 2015 by Wayland

Copyright © Wayland 2015

Wayland
338 Euston Road
London NW1 3BH

Wayland Australia
Level 17/207 Kent Street
Sydney NSW 2000

All rights reserved.
Series editor: Elizabeth Brent

Produced by Tall Tree Ltd
Editor: Jon Richards
Designers: Ed Simkins and Jonathan Vipond

Dewey classification: 355.4-dc23

ISBN: 978 0 7502 8761 6
ebook: 978 0 7502 8762 3
Printed in Malaysia

Wayland is a division of Hachette
Children's Books, an Hachette UK company.
www.hachette.co.uk

10 9 8 7 6 5 4 3 2 1

Picture credits
WIKI/Adam Cuerden/Library of Congress, shutterstock/Kamira, WIKI/Public domain, shutterstock/Tatiana Popova, GETTY/Massimo Taparelli d'Azeglio, WIKI/Public domain, GETTY/ Time Life Pictures/Getty, shutterstock/Neftali/ Shutterstock.com, shutterstock/rook76/Shutterstock. com, GETTY/Leemage/Getty, shutterstock/Neftali / Shutterstock.com, WIKI/Public domain, WIKI/Public domain, shutterstock/Bikeworldtravel, shutterstock/ Neftali/Shutterstock.com, WIKI/Public domain, WIKI/ Adam Cuerden/Library of Congress, WIKI/Public domain, GETTY/Paul Popper/Popperfoto/Getty, shutterstock/photoiconix, shutterstock/Keith Tarrier, WIKI/Public domain, shutterstock/lexan, WIKICreative Commons Attribution-Share Alike 3.0 Unported license, WIKI/Public domain, WIKI/Public domain

GET EPIC!

Cross the globe on a journey of discovery and learn about some of the greatest events from the natural and human world. Read about the most epic migrations, battles, empires and explorers the world has ever seen.

EPIC ANIMAL MIGRATIONS
12 EPIC JOURNEYS — OVER LAND, SEA AND AIR
CAMILLA DE LA BÉDOYÈRE
9780750287579

EPIC BATTLES
12 EPIC BATTLES — ON LAND, SEA AND IN THE AIR
ROB COLSON
9780750287616

EPIC EMPIRES
12 EPIC EMPIRES — ANCIENT AND MODERN
PHILIP STEELE
9780750287555

EPIC EXPLORERS
12 EPIC JOURNEYS — ACROSS LAND, SEA AND SPACE
PHILIP STEELE
9780750287593